essentials

Remembering Names and Faces

D0088668

Time-saving books that teach specific skills to busy people, focusing on what really matters; the things that make a difference – the *essentials*. Other books in the series include:

Making Great Presentations

Pass Your Practical Driving Test

Speaking in Public

Succeeding at Interviews

Moving House with Feng Shui

Sell Your Home Using Feng Shui

Getting Started on the Internet

Writing Great Copy

Making the Best Man's Speech

Feeling Good for No Good Reason

Making the Most of Your Time

Responding to Stress

For full details please send for a free copy of the latest catalogue. See back cover for address.

The things that really matter about

Remembering Names and Faces

Dr Harry Alder

ESSENTIALS

First published in 2000 by
How To Books Ltd, 3 Newtec Place,
Magdalen Road, Oxford OX4 1RE, United Kingdom
Tel: (01865) 793806   Fax: (01865) 248780
email: info@howtobooks.co.uk
www.howtobooks.co.uk

All rights reserved. No part of this work may be reproduced or stored
in an information retrieval system (other than for purposes of review),
without the express permission of the publisher in writing.

© **Copyright 2000 Dr Harry Alder**

British Library Cataloguing in Publication Data.
A catalogue record for this book is available from
the British Library.

Edited by Kelly Davis
Cover design by Shireen Nathoo Design
Produced for How To Books by Deer Park Productions
Cover copy by Sallyann Sheridan
Typeset by Anneset, Weston-super-Mare, Somerset
Printed and bound by Hillman Printers, Frome, Somerset

NOTE: The material contained in this book is set out in good faith for
general guidance and no liability can be accepted for loss or expense
incurred as a result of relying in particular circumstances on
statements made in the book. Laws and regulations are complex and
liable to change, and readers should check the current position with
the relevant authorities before making personal arrangements.

ESSENTIALS *is an imprint of*
How To Books

Contents

Preface

Remembering names and faces presents a problem for many people. In some cases this is no more serious than the occasional embarrassing moment. In other cases it brings with it frustration, annoyance and intense anxiety. When your job involves working with people, remembering names and faces can be a major factor in achieving success. For every one of us it is a skill worth acquiring.

However you rate your memory, remembering people's names and faces can become a natural, pleasurable part of your life. We all have the innate ability to do this. Armed with the basic memory principles and simple DIY mind skills you will learn in this book, you will soon start to surprise yourself, and gain new confidence when interacting with other people.

You need not confine your attention to names and faces. Once acquired, these mind skills will help you in other areas of your life, such as your business or career, academic achievements, hobbies, social interests, and self-improvement. There is simply no limit to what you can accomplish with a standard issue brain. It's never too late to start, and the fun comes as a bonus.

Harry Alder

1 Getting Down to Basics

By following a few simple rules, and before learning any special techniques, you will dramatically improve your name-remembering skills.

5 things that really matter

1 HEARING THE PERSONS'S NAME

2 SPELLING THE PERSON'S NAME

3 REMARKING ON THE NAME

4 USING THE NAME IN YOUR FIRST MEETING

5 SAYING THE NAME WHEN YOU LEAVE

There are several proven techniques that can enable anyone to remember people's names. And you don't need a good memory or a special brain to learn them. Some of the techniques may be new to you. In this case, all you need is an open mind and a willingness to give them a try.

This chapter outlines five simple, commonsense rules that you can immediately apply, before learning the principles and special memory techniques covered in the rest of the book. You should notice an improvement straight away. In particular, you will notice your attitude and interest in people changing. The pleasure you get and the benefits you realise will motivate you to carry on learning. In that confident, positive, 'I can' frame of mind, you will soon master remembering people's names and faces. So let's get down to basics.

IS THIS YOU?

● I sometimes forget a name just moments after I have been introduced. ● If there are more than three or four people I don't even try to remember their names – it's a waste of time. ● It's so embarrassing not to be able to put a name to a face when I bump into an old acquaintance – even someone I used to know well. It is especially embarrassing when they immediately remember me. ● It would be so useful in my job if I could remember people's names easily.

① HEARING THE PERSON'S NAME

- **When you are introduced or you first meet, listen carefully and be sure to hear the person's name.** If you don't 'register' it in your memory there is not much chance of recalling it. You never 'remembered' it in the first place. (Listening is an important foundation to the memory skills you will learn later.)

- **If the person's name is not clear – which can often be the case in a noisy environment – ask them to repeat it.** This happens all the time and no one will be in the least offended. You can do it in the simplest way: 'Sorry you are . . . ?' or 'Let me get that right, you are . . . ?'

- **If you hear part of the name, just repeat what you *think* you heard. 'Sorry, you are Mel . . . ?'** The person will immediately finish it off for you, making it clearer.

- **If it's a common name like Bill or Joan, the chances are that you will easily hear it.** In that case just be sure to consciously hear it **inside**. That helps to **register** the name firmly in your mind.

- **If it seems natural to respond immediately to the person by name – 'Hello Joan' – so much the better.** It will help to register it in your memory. In any event, give your memory a sporting chance and get into the habit of consciously **hearing** any name you wish to remember.

People always have more interest in their own name than anyone else's. So, as well as helping you to remember, using a person's name is a 'hot-button' to get their attention and establish a favourable impression. It pays to hear the name right at the start.

 ## SPELLING THE PERSON'S NAME

- **Next, spell the person's name.** A lot of names have more than one spelling, and it is perfectly natural to ask 'Is that with two **t's**?' or 'is that **ie** or **ey**?' You can be sure that the person has been asked the same question many times and will be quite happy to 'spell it out' to anyone who shows an interest.

- **Knowing how to spell the person's name has great value.** Certain names are spelt wrongly all the time and it can be annoying. It is pleasing to have your name spelt correctly in a written communication from a person you have only met once. The sender will probably go up a notch in your estimation. Spelling a name will also help to establish your memory of it. It will then *mean* more than just a sound.

- **If you hear the name clearly and have no doubt about the spelling (say Smith, Jones, or White) you don't need to spell it out loud.** You may well remember the person's name better by doing so, but they will probably also remember you as stupid or illiterate. But, whatever the name, spell it anyway **to yourself**. Usually it is the most common names we forget, whereas unusual ones tend to stick in the mind.

- **Check which spelling the person uses**. Often different spellings apply to similar-sounding names (such as Johnston, Johnson, Johnstone; Blyth, Blythe; or Thomson, Thompson, Thomason). You can ask: 'Is that Thompson with a **p**?' 'Blythe with an **e**?' and so on. This shows that you are knowledgeable about different spelling, and, more importantly, it shows your interest in the person. In the case of common variants you don't need to spell out a name fully ('is that spelt M-c-P-h-e-r-s-o-n?'), or get the person to. Life is too short. You are not displaying name-spelling skills, just trying to remember the person's name.

- **If you don't hear the spelling right first time, repeat what you *think* you heard, and be ready to be corrected letter by letter**. The person will intuitively stop you at the first letter you get wrong, and will spell out the rest. Try it. Don't worry about strange, foreign-sounding spellings. They are more fun – just use the same process. In any event, the more you get a name wrong, the better you will remember it in the longer term. The extra concentration needed to register the spelling adds meaning to the name and makes it easier to recall.

Paradoxically, strange or unusual names are best as far as this rule is concerned. You have more reason to refer to the spelling. In such cases you can simply ask 'How do you spell that?'

Wishing to know how to spell a person's name also implies the possibility of a longer-term relationship. Its value may extend beyond the duration of a dinner party, training seminar or client meeting, when you know you just have to remember names for a couple of hours. Even a chance meeting can sometimes result in a beneficial relationship, so applying this simple rule can bring you big dividends in the future.

REMARKING ON THE NAME

- **Make some remark about the person's name.** In some of the above cases you will have already done this. But, regardless of whether you get to spell it out, there are all sorts of legitimate ways to bring the person's name into your initial conversation. Let's face it; if you know nothing about the person at all, you have to start somewhere. But religion, politics or sport can easily get you off on the wrong foot, and the weather tends to be somewhat overdone as a subject of small talk. Moreover, you **know** that the person is interested in their name, and will respond favourably to anyone who shares their interest.

- **Think of something that might suggest a remark about the name.** For instance, you may have an existing friend, work colleague or relative with the same or a similar name. 'Ha, that's my youngest daughter's [or grandmother's, or previous boss's – but not cat's] name'. Many names immediately bring someone or some thing to your mind, such as a rock star, sports personality, writer, politician, medieval king, tree (like Birch or Alder), flower, occupation (like Carpenter or Miller), or whatever. Provided you use them carefully, these associations can also lend themselves to 'smalltalk' remarks.

- **In other cases, the name might prompt you to think of a useful topic to further the conversation and build mutual rapport**. For example, 'wasn't there an Olympic swimmer called . . . [**say** the name – another chance to register it in your memory]?' Whether or not the person has any interest in swimming doesn't matter. They will surely know about the swimmer namesake, having heard the comment lots of times. If not, it doesn't matter anyway ('I must have been thinking of somebody else'). By then you have broken the ice, and created a memory association.

- **Always use common sense**. Especially avoid hackneyed remarks, puns or a reference to a household name entertainer or sportsperson having the same name but with possible negative connotations – 'Oh, any relation to . . .?' Such a remark can be very offputting. If you own name attracts silly comments you will know how little they do for first impressions.

- **The main point is that remarking on the name, on any reasonable pretext, helps to imprint it in your memory**.

Any mental 'note', just like spelling the name, adds meaning and memorability. Although it is preferable, memory-wise, to make your remark out loud, there is also plenty of benefit in remarks you make to yourself.

 USING THE NAME IN YOUR FIRST MEETING

- **Always try to use the person's name during your first meeting**. If this is a fleeting introduction, you will have already followed the earlier rules, and **heard**, **said**, **spelt**

and **remarked on** the name. That may be about all you can squeeze in before saying a hasty farewell. But, even in a very brief meeting, there is usually a chance to slot the person's name into your actual communication. This is particularly true if you are chatting 'one to one', or to an individual within a group, rather than to or within the whole group.

- **Use the name in a way you are comfortable with, and that does not sound contrived.** 'But don't you think, Helen, . . .'. Using the name in a natural, unaffected way will endear you (maybe unconsciously) to the person. We all like to be addressed by name, and tend to warm to a person who uses it in a genuine way.

- **The more times you use the name, the more firmly it will be imprinted in your memory.** In fact, after using a person's name a few times it becomes more difficult to **forget** it than to remember it. If repeating the name too often sounds affected, you can say the person's name **to yourself.** For instance, 'When I was there last – (Barry Barry Barry [to yourself – it just takes a moment between words]) – they weren't even built' and so on.

 SAYING THE NAME WHEN YOU LEAVE

- **Finally, say the person's name when you part.** The moment we meet is when we pay (even momentarily) our best attention. This is why it's so important to register the name as soon as possible. It's also a fact that we remember recent things best. So, saying the name once more on parting is another good way of repeating and thus reinforcing it in your memory.

- **Again, do this in a way that sounds natural.** 'Good to meet you, Helen'. 'See you soon, Barry.'

Once you have followed the basic rules a few times they will become second nature. Soon you will be in the habit of paying attention and remembering people. In the long run, creating useful habits is the easiest, most effective way to get what you want. And the habit of remembering names is one of the best examples. So it's worth getting the basics right.

MAKING WHAT MATTERS WORK FOR YOU

✔ Apply these rules at the first opportunity, whether socially or at work. Start now.

✔ Apply the rules **every time** you are in a name-remembering situation. Even if you don't need to remember the names of everybody you meet, you will do yourself a favour by boosting mental skills that you can use when you need to.

✔ Notice how easy and enjoyable it is and congratulate yourself on each success.

✔ Each week, think back to the people you have met, and see if you can quickly recall their names. This not only helps to imprint the names further in your memory, but does wonders for your self-esteem and overall memory skills.

2 Making Memories

*Applying a few simple principles
will take you a long way towards
solving memory problems.*

2

things that
really matter

1 WE REMEMBER 'FIRST' AND 'LASTS'

2 REPETITION REINFORCES MEMORY

Two simple memory principles explain why we remember
some things better than others.

These principles concern the way we **actually** remember
things, based on research carried out over many years. By
understanding and applying these key principles, you will
remember names and faces intuitively and easily.

To see some characteristics of memory in action, try this
simple experiment. Which of the following names do you
think you would remember most easily? Spend a few
moments looking at them, then turn away and see how
many you can remember.

**Brodie, Currie, Garrett, White, Dunrad, Rainbow, Drury,
Hartnell, Garlick**.

Write down the names you recalled before carrying on to
learn these memory principles.

① WE REMEMBER 'FIRST' AND 'LASTS'

When we learn or experience anything we remember what comes first and what comes last better than what comes in between.

THE PRIMACY EFFECT

The first word on a list, the first person you are introduced to in a group, the opening moments of a speech or presentation, the beginning of a letter, meeting, book, year, journey, day, sermon, or whatever, will often stick in your mind. Writers, for instance, know the importance of the start of a book, and performers the start of a performance. Our attention is usually highest at the beginning of a communication, event or new experience. Hence the immediate, and often lasting, first impression we sometimes get when we meet a new person, even if it changes afterwards. You can usually remember the first time you met a close friend, or important person in your life, or even the first words they spoke, after many years.

This memory principle, known as the **primacy effect**, applies in all sorts of situations. Perhaps you remembered 'Brodie', the first name on the above list. You can apply this basic memory characteristic specifically to remembering names and faces.

THE RECENCY EFFECT

We also tend to remember whatever comes last (and this is known as the **recency effect**). Because it is the most recent event, we have simply had less time to forget it. For instance, we tend to remember the closing words of a speech, the ending of a story, the grand finale of a performance or the punchline of a joke.

This rule can also apply to the last person we are introduced to – sometimes that's the only one we manage to remember, especially if there are more than half a dozen people in the group.

For example, an interviewer usually remembers the first impression a candidate creates. In a similar way, she will tend to remember the first person on a shortlist of interviewees. Her attention is better at the start of an afternoon's interviewing, and also, briefly, at the start of each interview. She may flag as the afternoon wears on and, in any case, can only 'carry so much in her head'.

She may also recall the closing moments of an interview. Often, at this point, her first (intuitive) impressions are either confirmed or corrected. She has to think about making a decision, and, once again, pay attention.

Similarly, she can usually recall the last interviewee on a shortlist – the most recent in her memory. This usually means that the first and last candidates are remembered better than those who come in between. For better or worse, they get the lion's share of consideration in the decision process that follows.

Likewise, the beginning and end of each interview are remembered best, so the performance of a candidate is particularly critical at these points.

*You can make use of these principles when interviewing or being interviewed. As an interviewer, you can, for instance, pay special attention to what goes 'in between', thus correcting for **primacy and recency bias**. As a candidate, you can ensure that you make an opening and closing impact. Interviews are just one of many examples of the importance of these memory principles.*

REPETITION REINFORCES MEMORY

Repetition plays a big part in memory and learning. It is the proven method for learning multiplication tables, memorising lines for a play and any long-term memory task that requires accuracy and instant recall. This is why things we learnt 'parrot fashion' as children usually stay in our memory for many years. However, we also apply this principle as adults all the time – when we **repeat** to ourselves a telephone number, or **repeat** a car registration number, or **repeat** the directions we are given to find a street in an unfamiliar neighbourhood. When we want to remember something for a short while without writing it down, **repetition** usually does the trick. And the more we **repeat** the memory, the more it 'sinks in' and becomes a long-term memory.

This principle is widely understood and used, for example by television advertisers and communicators generally. It can also apply to remembering people's names and faces. Most people can recall the names of personalities who regularly appear on television better than some of their own personal and business acquaintances. Even when we are not interested in the person or subject in question, **repetition** will usually carve out a permanent memory.

You may have realised that these 'first', 'last' and 'repetition' memory principles also feature in the basic rules you met in Chapter 1. Let me **repeat** them:

- Hear and say the name at the beginning (**primacy**).

- Make some remark about the name (**repetition**).

- Use the name in the course of a first meeting (**repetition**).

- Use the name as you leave (**recency**).

You don't need any special skills to apply these basic rules. The memory principles in this chapter, on which they are based, simply reflect some of the ways your brain actually processes memories.

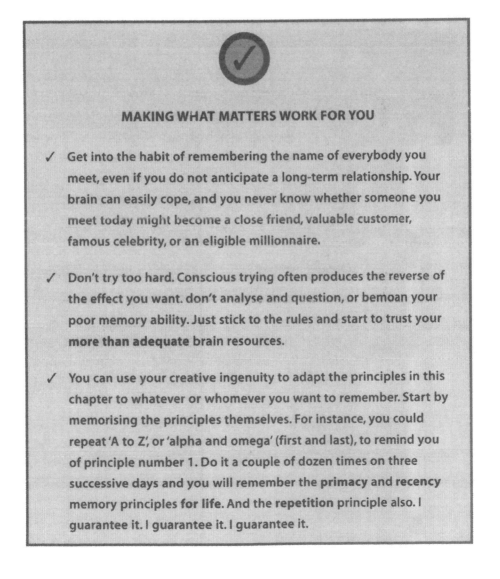

MAKING WHAT MATTERS WORK FOR YOU

✓ Get into the habit of remembering the name of everybody you meet, even if you do not anticipate a long-term relationship. Your brain can easily cope, and you never know whether someone you meet today might become a close friend, valuable customer, famous celebrity, or an eligible millionnaire.

✓ Don't try too hard. Conscious trying often produces the reverse of the effect you want. don't analyse and question, or bemoan your poor memory ability. Just stick to the rules and start to trust your **more than adequate** brain resources.

✓ You can use your creative ingenuity to adapt the principles in this chapter to whatever or whomever you want to remember. Start by memorising the principles themselves. For instance, you could repeat 'A to Z', or 'alpha and omega' (first and last), to remind you of principle number 1. Do it a couple of dozen times on three successive days and you will remember the **primacy** and **recency** memory principles **for life**. And the **repetition** principle also. I guarantee it. I guarantee it. I guarantee it.

3 Seeing Sense

Names are much easier to remember if they mean something – now you can learn how to create 'memorable meaning'.

3

things that
really matter

1 **CREATING A MEANING FOR A NAME**

2 **USING YOUR VISUAL SENSE**

3 **UNDERSTANDING 'MULTI-SENSORY' MEANING**

The human brain likes to understand and classify things. Like books in a library, our experiences of things and people have to fit somewhere in our mental 'catalogue'. Unless they **belong** somewhere, they can't be retrieved when needed.

Something that has no meaning, including a person's name, cannot be retrieved (remembered). It has not been properly recorded and classified in your brain, so your brain doesn't know what to look for. Once a name has meaning it occupies a mental pigeonhole where you can always locate it when you need to. It becomes a 'proper' memory.

Which of the following shortlist of words would you find it easier to remember?

LIST 1
Crift
Jerv

Sarll

Pebe

Hial

LIST 2

Gentlemen

Fairweather

Overnight

Rhinoceros

Pudding

Most people would find the first list harder – because the words, for most of us, have no meaning. Spoken words, including names, are just very sophisticated, complex noises unless they mean something. The words in the second list, although they contain twice as many letters, are easier to remember, because they have meaning.

ⓘ CREATING A MEANING FOR A NAME

To remember a name it has to have a meaning. In many cases names that at first mean nothing will mean something if you think about them for a few moments, especially if you intend to remember them. However, the process may not be fast enough to avoid the embarrassment of forgetting a person's name when you are introduced to them socially or at work. That's when the skills you are about to learn come into play.

'Registering' meaning in the brain happens automatically. We **interpret** words or experiences, **make sense** of the world around us and continuously create memories.

Recalling memories also happens automatically. You don't usually think about how or whether you will remember what you experience moment by moment. You manage to find your way to work, for instance, without a street map. You recognise the person at the next desk without taking along a photograph, and remember their name without checking in a filofax. Most of our remembering doesn't take 'a moment's (conscious) thought'. With the staggering brain capacity we have, that's the way it should be.

To create a meaning you simply **think** about a name. Applying the five basic rules from Chapter 1 forces you to do this. Something 'comes to mind'. By being more **conscious** of this process, and **confident** in your brain capability, you can improve your memory skills.

② USING YOUR VISUAL SENSE

The visual sense is the dominant sense and a key to remembering names and faces. A 'picturable' meaning is easier to remember than an abstract, intangible name. Vision is the most complex sense, and physically takes up the biggest sensory processing part of your brain. We all have more than enough mental hardware, and we can run our own memory 'software'.

The name 'White' is a 'visual' word because you can **visualise** the colour white. You can **picture** something white in your mind's eye. For instance, white might bring to mind (literally):

- snow in Vermont

- George's Porsche

- your hometown of Whitehaven

- or the white gloves you wore as a bridesmaid.

In such cases 'white' **means** more than a colour, and certainly more than a word or a name. For you, a picturable association with 'white' will trigger the name 'White'. 'Colour names' are just one example of picturable names that are easy to remember.

Similarly, you can **imagine** a rainbow, or something coloured like a rainbow or that reminds you of, a rainbow. The names White and Rainbow both appeared on the list in the previous chapter. If you remembered these names it may have been because they were 'picturable'. Visual names like these are usually easier to remember than names you cannot picture.

The more 'picturable' or 'imaginable' a word, the more meaning it has, and the easier it will be to remember. Likewise, you can easily visualise a rhinoceros or your favourite pudding (in the second list above), and recall memories that involved these kinds of picturable things.

You can visualise consciously. It is a mental skill that you can improve with practice. Many people find it useful for relaxing, goal-setting and learning. It has a large part to play in memory, as we give things and people picturable meanings.

 UNDERSTANDING 'MULTI-SENSORY' MEANING

To experience the 'real' world, we use not only sight, but all five senses. So if the **inner** name association is multi-sensory – evoking sights, sounds, feelings, and maybe tastes and smells – so much the better. It is more **real**. Names with a 'multi-sensory' meaning make for better long-term memories and are easiest to recall. For example, the **feel** of cold, powdery snow will create more than just a 'picture' of 'white' snow. And the **sound** of a white Porsche 911 accelerating will be easier to recall than just the name White.

For most people, Currie (a name which also appeared on the list in the previous chapter) has little or no meaning if you don't happen to know someone by that name. But for many people the smell and taste of **curry** will stir the senses and be easy to imagine and remember. Just by **thinking** the 'curry' meaning of Currie, you give it instant, sensory meaning. Names with sensory meanings like this are sometimes harder to forget than to remember. If you remembered the name Currie from the list in the last chapter, it may well have conjured up some sensory association for you. For us to remember a name it has to have **some** sensory meaning, even though we are rarely conscious of the process.

All memories, along with thoughts and imaginings, are multi-sensory, of course. They simply mirror real-life experience. But some are more **multi**-sensory than others. That is, they are easily recalled in **several** senses. For example, the names Bell or Trumpeter are likely to conjure up **sounds**, which, along with **images**, form part of their sensory meaning. Similarly, you can **hear** as well as **see** the wolf that Mrs Woolfe brings to mind, and **feel** as well as **see** the silk that the name Silke evokes.

Conversely, some memories are more **sensory** than others, even though they do not evoke **multi**-sensory associations. That is, the sense or senses they **do** comprise are strong and vivid – more memorable, or 'larger than life'. For instance, the slightest smell or taste can instantly take us back to a strong, childhood memory, almost as though we were reliving the experience. So the more **multi** and **sensory** its meaning, the easier a name will be to recall.

You can consciously develop what is termed *sensory acuity*. Artists, musicians, stonemasons, heart surgeons, architects and wine-tasters, for instance, tend to develop strongly developed senses. This happens through application and a lot of practice (repetition). Not only can they discriminate between different images, sounds or feelings *externally* in the normal course of their work, but they can also create or manipulate these *internally*.

The architect, for instance, can see more than a two-dimensional drawing, and the sculptor can see more than a block of stone. Their true skill involves both internal and external senses. Both can be trained. And these are innate skills that we all have. By using them you can start to add lifelike, multi-sensory meaning to the things and people you want to remember.

Different names will 'register' with different people in different ways and with different meanings. Each will evoke very different associations, images, sounds and feelings. We can all draw on a lifetime of richly varied experiences, and these create the unique associations we make. To remember a name, it doesn't matter what particular meaning it has for you – the content, if you like – as long as that meaning triggers the name when you want to recall it. What matters is the **nature** of the memory, and the **process** of recording and recalling it.

The test for a name you want to remember is:

● Does the name have **sensory** meaning?

● Can you see it, hear it, feel it, smell it, taste it?

● Or, to put it another way, can you clearly **imagine** the name as **more** than just a word?

To create memorable name meanings you just need to use your imagination, which we all have in abundance. In the following chapters you will learn how to find a meaning for any name.

MAKING WHAT MATTERS WORK FOR YOU

✓ Start giving a **picturable meaning** to every name you hear or read. You will soon be able to do this with hardly a moment's (conscious) thought.

✓ When faced with remembering a new name, pay **imaginative, sensory** attention. Bring your heart as well as your head into the process.

✓ When following the five basic rules in Chapter 1, add a picturable, sensory meaning at the same time as you think or say the name. This will lock them both into a mental pigeonhole so that you cannot recall one without the other. It can be the key to making a name unforgettable.

4 Making Meaning Memorable

Once you can find meanings for names, remembering them will no longer be a problem.

2

**things that
really matter**

1 IDENTIFYING 'BUILT IN' MEANING

2 MAKING EACH NAME MEMORABLE

Some names have meaning and some don't – or don't seem to. And a lot fall somewhere in between. Some names may be unfamiliar **as names** (of people). They nevertheless have meaning because the word itself, or the sound of the word, reminds you of a thing – a flower, animal or whatever. Something comes **to your mind** when you hear the name. For example, you may not know anyone by the name of Field or Singer, but these names nonetheless have picturable, sensory meanings of the kind we met in Chapter 3.

Other names have meaning just because we already know someone with that name. For instance, you might associate the name Johnson with a neighbour, a schoolteacher from many years ago, or Johnson's floor polish. Apart from this association, the name is just a word, without an obvious meaning of its own (like Field and Singer).

You can now start to apply the memory principles you

have learnt to remembering names. For memory purposes, there are essentially three kinds of names:

- **Names that have an intrinsic, or 'built-in' meaning**. The **word itself** – like Field, Singer or Rainbow – can easily be pictured.

- **Names that have no intrinsic meaning but are nonetheless familiar** – because you know or know of someone with that name. In this case the name itself, rather than what you associate with it, has meaning. We can call these 'familiar' names.

- **Names that do not suggest any meaning**. No picture comes to mind. The name seems hard to remember. These tend to create the most memory problems.

The 'colour names' that we met in the previous chapter, fall into the first category – names with a 'built-in' meaning. Even if you can only recall that a person's name is a colour ('let me think, was it Brown, or White . . . ?) you will probably soon make the connection. However, a colour may 'mean, more than just a colour. It usually has associations – whatever red, green etc **brings to your mind**. For instance, a particular green carpet; a colleague's red coffee mug; the white blouse that didn't fit last time; aunt Rosie's silver hair, and so on.

① IDENTIFYING 'BUILT-IN' MEANING

In this chapter, we will consider the first category – names with an intrinsic meaning. A picturable name (whether it is a colour, an animal, vegetable or mineral, or anything you can see in real life) is far easier for your brain to handle than an abstract, intangible name.

Moreover, you can easily **give** a meaning – an added, or different meaning – to an already picturable word. For instance, you can imagine a black hole, blue blood, a pink panther, or a beige pullover. We can all unlock from our imagination an unlimited number of such 'picturable' meanings. Any one of those meanings can provide the mental pigeonhole that makes a name easy to recall.

Although it may not seem so at first, there are hundreds of names with a 'built-in' meaning. With a little practice you can soon create a sizeable mental database of name meanings without hurting your brain at all. Those names will probably cover a large percentage of the names you are likely to need to remember.

The name 'Sparrow', for example, conjures up an image of a sparrow. If you met a Mr Sparrow you would probably remember his name a week later, having associated him in some way with a sparrow. How many of this type of name (the first of the three types we identified) can you think of? To bring names with a meaning to mind, it helps to think of categories. For instance:

- **towns** (e.g. York, Bedford, Huntingdon, Chester)

- **trade or professions** (e.g. Parsons, Butcher)

- **animals** (e.g. Lyons, Deere)

Each category is replete with people's names. By thinking of categories (with meaning) you will automatically think of names (with meaning). Like colours – another category – these broad classifications are easily picturable in some way, and will, in turn, help to trigger picturable names of that sort.

Below I have listed the sorts of categories that easily

suggest images, and names within each category. I just picked names from a telephone directory and allocated them to the categories they seemed to belong to. These illustrate the hundreds of names that are picturable, and thus amenable to being remembered. Some names have several associations, so you usually have a choice of meaning.

Some of the names I have included might have little or no meaning **to you** (at least at first sight). But, conversely, you will probably think of other names in each category that have meaning for you but not for me. For memory purposes, meaning is **whatever comes to your mind**. It need be neither logical nor literal – just **imaginable**. This immediate association will trigger the name whenever you need to remember it.

For our immediate purposes, spelling doesn't matter. I have highlighted some of the spellings, just to make the association (I made) clearer. I have also shown common variants of a name, often with different endings, which further multiply the number of names with a meaning.

You may find that some of the name associations don't strictly belong in the categories. That doesn't matter. The categories just help you to instinctively think of more picturable and thus 'rememberable names'. With practice, you will start doing this quickly and intuitively. Most of these are family surnames, but you can treat first names in the same way. Try adding a few names of your own to each category:

- **Trades/professions**: Turner, Porter, Shepherd, Plummer, Foreman, Barber, Carpenter, Butler, Parsons, Brewer,

Farmer, Mason, Marshall, Carver, Potter, Cobbler, Tanner

- **Trees**: Beech, Alder, Palm(-er, -erston), Ash(ley)

- **Towns**: London, Bradford, Warwick, York, Carlisle

- **Animals**: Fox, Colt, Hart, Wolfe

- **Birds**: Rob(b)ins(-on), Nightingale, Parrotte, Feather(stone), Swift(man)

- **Tools/artefacts**: Hammers, Bell, Saw(yer), Hook(er), Keyes, Potts, Mallett

- **Flowers**: Heather(ton), Rose(well, -man, -ly), Lilley

- **Fishes**: Roach, Herring, Fish, Newt(on)

- **Cars**: Carr, Ford, Bentley, Rolls, Royce, Morris, Austin, Plymouth (also a town)

- **Countries/regions**: Welsh, Franc(is), French, English, Germaine, North(umberland), Albany, South(-wark, -well, -worth, -am), Georg(ia), Virginia, Edmonton, Victoria, East(-man), West(-on, -ward, -wood)

- **Money**: Coyne, Penn(e)y, Farthing, Cash, Frank(s)(-lin), Go(u)ld, Silver(-man, -stone)

- **Weather/seasons**: Snow, Raine (or Rayner), Summers (or Sommers), Winters, Storm, March, May, Day(-ton), Weeks(s), Fyne, Cold(well)

- **Titles**: Baron, Lord, Prince(s), Bishop, Knight (-ley), King, Queen, Squires, Earl

- **Natural features**: Banks, Hill, Rivers, Star(r), Rock(er, -man, well), Burns, Shore, Wood(-man, -all, -head, -ley, -ruff, etc) Ford, Field, Moore, Water(s), Marsh(-all), Mount(batten), Moone

- **Food**: Berger, Rice, Fry (-er), Curry, Bacon, Corn(hill), Wheat(ley)

- **Man-made features**: Bridges, House(man), Ho(l)mes, Barn(es)(-ey, -aby, -staple), Wall, Towers, Fountain, Welles, Pitts, Road(e)s or Rhodes, Graves, Parkes, Gates, Lane, Post(-er), Dor(an)

- **Fruit**: Lemmon, Appel(man), Plum(mer), Berry, Cherry, Pear(son)

- **Mineral**: Gold(-water, -man), Iron(side), Silver, Diamond, Rock(-er, -erman, -well), Flint, (Living-)Stone, Sand(-s, -man, -ers, -erson)

- **Body features**: Legge, Hand(s)(-el, -ley), Harte, Foot, Arm(strong), Palm(er), Chest(er)

- **Monarchs**: Mary, William, Ann, Henry, King(sley), Queen, Elizabeth, Tudor, Windsor

- **Sport**: Bowles(-er), Cricket or Crockett, Tennys(on), Player

- **Measures**: Ince (inch), Short, Long, Low(e), Waite (weight), Little, Foot, Mile(s), Stone, (Hard)acre, Yard(ley)

- **Music/musicians**: Harper, Player, Drum(-mer, -ond), Piper, Bell, Carroll, Singer, Bowes, Bass(-ey, -ett)

- **Weapons**: Gunn, Arrowe, Lance, Grenade

- **Character/traits**: Noble, Good(e)(-man, -ing, -enough), Hope, Strong, Dowdy, Frett, Sage, Rich, Love(joy), Cryer

- **Materials**: Steele, Iron(side), Mettle, Cotton, Glass, Cloth(ier)

You will probably think of more and more names as you add categories. Even the **categories** can run into hundreds/ For instance, what about:

- vegetables

- machines

- planets

- writers

- precious stones

- footballers

- medical terms

- legal terms

- travel

- religion

- fiction

- rivers

- poetry

- clothing

- games

- plants

- or book titles?

Every name that comes to your mind has a **meaning** – or you would not be able to classify it in a 'meaning category'. And once a name has a meaning, you will remember it better, whatever the context or situation. You don't need to memorise these names, although you can't stop a few sticking in your mind. Just **by going through the process** you will acquire the basic ability to identify name meanings – a foundation skill for remembering names and faces.

The memory principles are just the same for first and middle names. They fall into the same categories of 'names with a meaning', 'familiar' and 'no meaning'.

At a first meeting, you will usually only have to remember either the first name or the surname. This will depend on whether it is an informal 'first name' occasion, or more formal (as when meeting a potential client for the first time). Where you need to remember a whole group, you will not be expected to register more than one name per person. Many new first names will already be familiar to you. You may know several Johns and Susans, for instance.

If you do need to remember both first and last names at an initial meeting, you have the basic skills you need to do that. Just make a **picturable connection.** For instance, if your picture for Chris is a cross, and you visualise a white flag for White, your memory picture for a Chris White can be a white flag with a cross on it.

 MAKING EACH NAME MEMORABLE

As we have seen, multi-sensory thoughts, or 'representations' of 'external' phenomena, are best for remembering. That's the way we recall a favourite holiday – **specific memories**, with sights, sounds, feelings, smells and tastes.

In making a familiar name 'multi-sensory', you can strengthen, add to or change its meaning in different ways. For instance, consider a Mrs Fairweather. You might associate her, not just with fair weather (rather than the name Fairweather), but also with a specific spot in an actual place on a particular holiday in glorious, balmy weather. That is, **specific, real** fair weather. By making a meaning more tangible or vivid, you will strengthen the name association and remember it better. In fact, you can use your imagination to tweak any name association in any way, to any degree, to make it unforgettable.

Similarly, you can **create** a strong memory association by adding a **different** meaning. In effect, you can **out-sense** the 'intrinsic' name meaning that comes to mind with something more graphic and memorable – particularly if you had to struggle to make any association. In this case the stronger association will override any existing one.

For example, if you wish, you can imagine Mrs Fairweather sunbathing on a desert satellite about 15 miles from the sun – hot, sure, but unforgettably fair weather! Or you could visualise Mrs Fairweather's bushy eyebrows as hawthorn hedgerows, graced with birdsong and an evocative fragrance, outside a picturesque village (in fair weather, if you like). In other words, by one means or another, you can make a name **unforgettable**.

With a little imagination, you can even give abstract or non-sensory words a sensory meaning. You need never be stuck with a bland, hard-to-remember name. For instance, Ms Short can be visualised as a short straw, a short piece of string, shortbread, shorthand, or short anything. Mr Waite can be a brass **weight** or a 'Please Wait' notice in the doctor's surgery. The raw material of memories is **sensory**. That's what strong memories are made of. And that is the key to remembering names and faces.

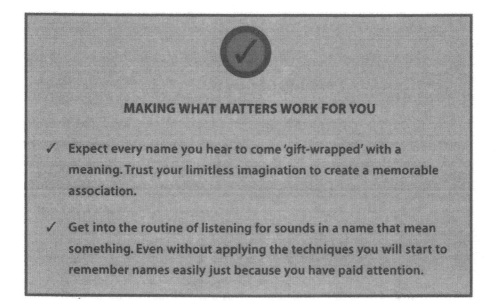

MAKING WHAT MATTERS WORK FOR YOU

✓ Expect every name you hear to come 'gift-wrapped' with a
    meaning. Trust your limitless imagination to create a memorable
    association.

✓ Get into the routine of listening for sounds in a name that mean
    something. Even without applying the techniques you will start to
    remember names easily just because you have paid attention.

5 It's Who You Know

Names you already know are an important memory resource that you can use for remembering other names.

2

things that
really matter

1 USING YOUR FAMILIAR NAME RESOURCES
2 CHOOSING THE STRONGEST NAME ASSOCIATION

The second category identified at the start of the previous chapter includes names of people you know or know of, brand names and suchlike. We can lump these together as 'familiar' names. They may be real, such as your new niece, Jodie, or fictional, such as character in a novel. These names have meaning by virtue of the people (like Jodie or Robinson Crusoe) or things (like Cadbury's chocolate) they belong to. Like names with an intrinsic meaning, they are easy to remember. Because they are familiar, they **already** have meaning – whatever the owner of the name **brings to mind** – **in addition** to any intrinsic meaning they may have (for instance, you might already know a real Mr Field). In this way, familiar names may well give you more than one meaning to use for memory purposes.

(I) USING YOUR FAMILIAR NAME RESOURCES

Some of these familiar names will 'register' the moment you see the face, or think about the person or character in any way. Others, such as the name of an entertainer, politician or a distant relative, might take a few moments and a little memory jogging.

You may not want to remember the name of a politician, character in an old film, or your second cousin, of course. Maybe you are happy enough remembering just friends, family and work colleagues – and any people you meet who may fall into that category. That's fine, but bear in mind that **any** familiar name (that you can easily remember from the face) can be a memory peg for remembering new people **with the same name**. And you won't damage your brain, feel pain, or run out of neural storage space, however many familiar names you store in your 'familiar name' mental database.

The more familiar names you can identify, the easier it will be to remember the names of new people you meet. Who we remember and who we don't usually happens unconsciously and haphazardly, and sometimes our memory lets us down. However, with your new memory skills, you can create and manage whatever size personal 'portfolio' of familiar names you want – however infrequently you may need to recall them.

You can probably come up with a sizeable 'familiar' list. And thinking of different 'familiar' **categories** will remind you of familiar names. For example, think about:

- television personalities

- sportspeople

- personal friends

- colleagues

- relatives

- children's friends

- neighbours

- writers

- actors

- artists

- customers

- suppliers

- singers

- politicians

- school and college friends

- fictional characters in novels

- casual acquaintances

- companies (such as Dixons or Marks & Spencer)

- products (such as Johnson's baby cream or Wilkinson Sword razor blades)

How many categories are relevant to you? And how many 'familiar' names can you think of in each category? For many people this group of names runs into hundreds. A keen soccer fan, for instance, will not only reel off the names of players in the leading league teams, but also coaches and managers, television sports presenters, newspaper commentators, retired players and so on. Then there are football clubs, like Sunderland, Ranger(s), Cobblers, Luton, Everton (all people's names). And those examples are based on just **one** interest or hobby, of which a person may have several. An avid reader, for instance, will also know scores of fictional characters, as well as authors.

 CHOOSING THE STRONGEST NAME ASSOCIATION

Normally, remembering your personal shortlist of names of close friends, family, colleagues, favourite singers and so on is not a problem, although it may have been when you first made acquaintance. Names in this category, for whatever reason, have already established a mental peg in your mind.

By linking a name to a known person, you make it instantly picturable through that connection. You can then use the same association to remember another person with that name. Any 'image' you have of the familiar person, concerning their job, nationality, voice, mannerisms and suchlike will suffice. The stronger the name association, the better it will work as a memory resource. It need not be the person's face. For instance, you might not recognise Dickens' Oliver Twist in a crowd, but you can probably imagine him 'asking for more', or in some other role or image, and link that image to the Mr Oliver you want to remember. Choose what, for you, is the most memorable name association.

For example, if a new client has the same name as your brother-in-law, you can probably link them together in a way other than their name. Maybe they are both accountants, or both tall, both wear glasses, both have a bald patch, of similar age, both ex-military and so on. Whatever comes to your mind when you think about the brother-in-law connection **while looking at the client**, will provide a link. Just be sure to apply the basic rules you learnt in Chapter 1.

In the same way, if a Mrs Cartwright on your 'familiar' list is, or was, a schoolteacher, you might picture her in a classroom, writing with chalk on a blackboard, using a specific, familiar expression or mannerism and tone of voice. In short, make her **picturable** – or, more accurately, multi-sensory. As we have already seen, the more graphic and sensory the association, the better.

Use your imagination. The technique applies to names of **anyone** you know or know of. For instance, you might picture an entertainer singing a favourite song (thus adding an auditory element) at a specific performance; a sportsperson scoring a winning goal or point, at a **specific**, unforgettable final; a fictional character in their most popular role or situation; or a film actor saying a timeless line. The more memorable your familiar name 'package', the stronger the mental peg on which you can establish a memory link.

'Extended' familiar names (beyond your circle of family and friends) don't usually present memory problems. You remember them because they are familiar. In the case of fictional characters, real historical characters, famous leaders, or mega-stars, you probably won't need to remember them anyway other than at a pub quiz. You are unlike to bump into Shakespeare's Prince Hal in the corner shop.

However, you can use these names – hundreds of them – as the 'people association' to help you remember other people with the same name. The fact is that we don't come across many names, in everyday life, that we have never heard before. Once you have the know-how, you can decide when and how to apply your mental portfolio of familiar names.

When a name falls into both the first two categories (possessing an intrinsic meaning and a familiar name meaning), you have a further choice. For instance Fairweather reminds you of fair weather (or something to do with fair weather) and also (let's say) a Linda Fairweather you knew at college. You can use either meaning to remind you of a new Fairweather.

Similarly, you may know a real Mr Peacock, but the 'meaning' he evokes is as a person rather than a peacock. Or your boss's name is Gordon Field, but it would not occur to you to associate him with a field. You will then probably associate any other Field you meet with your boss ('oh, that's my boss's name'). The familiar name becomes a meaning peg upon which you can hang any other Field.

In such cases **one** of these associations (the 'familiar' meaning or the intrinsic or 'built-in' meaning) will be **stronger**, and come to your mind first. That is usually the best memory meaning to choose.

You don't have to rely on your memory for every thing or person you need to remember. Often a written note of somebody's name or a diary-type system will do the job perfectly well. It's just like using a shopping list, or a 'to do' list at work. In a meeting, seminar or group function, for instance, a simple diagram on a jotter, showing the layout of the seating, with names added to each position, may suffice. Often if you just listen to people addressing each other you can pencil in their names, so you don't need formal introductions.

*Written or other external memory props will probably only help for the duration of the meeting or function. That is fine if that's all you want. But if you want to remember a name permanently you should use the mind-picture technique you have learnt. Whatever system you use, the **conscious attention** you give to a person will probably solve your 'memory problem' anyway.*

Once you create a 'familiar name' resource, it's very easy to use it. Each association will readily come to mind as and when you need it – that is, **whenever** you hear the same or a similar name. You can then give your attention to names **without** any obvious meaning, which we will cover in the next chapter.

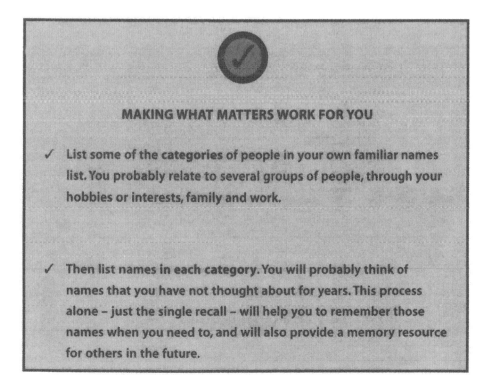

MAKING WHAT MATTERS WORK FOR YOU

✓ List some of the **categories** of people in your own familiar names list. You probably relate to several groups of people, through your hobbies or interests, family and work.

✓ Then list names in each category. You will probably think of names that you have not thought about for years. This process alone – just the single recall – will help you to remember those names when you need to, and will also provide a memory resource for others in the future.

6 Names Without a Meaning

Many names don't seem to have a meaning, but, using simple techniques, you can make any name easy to remember.

The third category identified in Chapter 4 is names without a meaning. These usually give us the most trouble. They are not readily picturable. And in the worst cases, such names are no more than a string of characters, no easier to remember than gibberish or a random telephone number you hear only once. However, with a little thought and imagination – which we can all muster when it suits our purpose – you can attach picturable meanings to many more names than you might have thought possible. As we have seen it's the associated picture that makes a name easy to remember.

① CREATING A MEANING FROM NOTHING

You cannot remember a name unless it has some 'sensory' meaning. However, if a name does not conjure up any meaning or association, you can **create** a meaning from the

name, or part of the name. When a name evokes no
instinctive mind picture, it simply means you have to **think**
(consciously) about the meaning. Look for, say, a **part** of the
word that has meaning, a word that sounds or looks similar,
a word that rhymes, and so on. Your brain is a meaning –
creation machine par excellence, and you can trust it to
come up with the goods. It sometimes seems to create a
meaning from nothing.

The name Haswell, for instance, is easily picturable when
you pick out the 'well'. In this case, you might imagine:

- looking down a deep well

- a well that spouts out water

- a well with a bucket and handle

- an oil well

- a well at an oasis

- an inkwell

- a 'get well' card

- a well-off person

- a stairwell

- a well of knowledge

Although a well may not **mean** the name Haswell,
nevertheless when you hear or read the name Haswell you
will think of 'well', in whatever way you cared to imagine it
when creating the association. Once you have input the
image, your brain makes the connection automatically.
Conversely, your 'well picture' will always bring the name
Haswell to mind – it's a two-way connection.

The well image has 'memory-meaning' for you (alone,

perhaps), and that's what you're after. For you, the name means 'well', and always will. From that point, if you meet anyone called Haswell, and follow the basic rules in the first chapter, you will intuitively make the association and remember them thereafter by it. A name that had no meaning now has a unique, vivid, easily rememberable meaning.

Creating meaning is a 'right brain', imaginative process that just takes a moment. You either make an intuitive association or you don't. If you take too long, the technique is not much use anyway in the context of meeting new people. You haven't failed. You just need a bit more practice using the mind techniques. These work best when you are not trying too hard, so don't stake your career on any specific memory technique. If you accept the odd mental block, they will occur less and less frequently.

 CREATING UNFORGETTABLE NAMES

The more outstanding and bizarre your mental image of a name, the better you will remember it. Anyone's imagination can create unforgettable memories. For instance, try **not** to think of a well when you think of Haswell, or Haswell when you think of a well. The harder you try, the more you will reinforce the association in your mind! Keep on trying (following the repetition principle you met in Chapter 2) and the name will become **unforgettable**.

Give it a try now. Create a memorable image for another common name – such as Jennings. Like Haswell (at first), this name also has no immediate meaning (unless you know a Jennings, in which case it will fall into your 'familiar' category). In this case you might visualise:

- jeans – wings (a pair of jeans sprouting wings or with a Wings designer label)

- a girl call Jenny, Jennifer or Jean carrying a basket of **things**, or wings, or singing (**thinging**) with a lisp (Jenn sings without the s's!)

- ginseng (the herb)

- gin inns (as in a hostelry)

If you can **imagine** something – anything – in response to a name, you can create the necessary memory link. This doesn't require intellect. The key mental skill – and we all possess it – is to **make a mind picture**. Having done this, you will have no trouble remembering the name.

Check out your Haswell and Jennings associations after an hour or so, then again the following morning. What images do the names instantly bring to mind? Each successful recall will make the name association increasingly indelible. More importantly, you will get to trust your own natural memory ability upon which the success of any technique will depend.

③ **CREATING NAME CLUES**

To make a memorable name association even **part of a name** will suffice (as we saw earlier with the name Haswell). You only need a clue – a link or association – not a literal match. There are lots of cases where part of a name has an easy association, such as Doran (door), or Drummond (drum) or Shelley (shell). In many cases, two or more parts of a name will have different associations. For example:

- **Roland** (roll, land)

- **Che(y)ney** (chain, knee)

- **Kissinger** (kiss, singer)

- **Tennyson** (tennis, son)

and so on. You can associate the name Roland with a 'roll' or a 'land' image and so on. Or you can make a mind picture that links both parts of a name. For example,

- **Roland**: a land (England, Australia, Iceland – take your pick) being rolled up (like a map)

- **Cheney**: Mr Cheney hanging from his knee by a chain

So, having been stuck for a meaning, you are now spoilt for choice. Now try making up your own 'double meanings' for Kissinger and Tennyson . . .

We saw earlier that a colour, shape, smell, taste or tune can instantly evoke a complete, realistic memory. In the same way, the tiniest memory clue, or caricature, is all you need to recall names. With such freedom, you can cut a few memory corners, and let your imagination run free. You will soon start to give meaning to just about any name you hear. In other words, your category one (names with a meaning) will include many more names than you first thought.

In practice, the name associations you make will probably be closer to literal meaning than some of the examples I have given (such as the ones for Jennings). That's fine, and you will easily make the link. You don't need to stick to tiny clues or subtle associations if you can create an apt association with a stronger link. However, by stretching your imagination to create the subtlest links, you will acquire the skill you need to make a picturable association – a meaning

– for **any** name you want to remember. Moreover, you will probably remember an outstanding or bizarre association more easily than a sensible, logical link that doesn't excite the imagination.

A chief executive I heard of was renowned for knowing the names of his hundreds of staff, however junior. In fact, he kept a simple card system in his desk drawer that just required a quick glance before someone came into his office. It had a powerful effect and he was liked and respected. Even when doing the round of the offices at Christmas he had little systems (much like the seating diagram in a meeting mentioned earlier). As it happened, many of the staff knew he didn't have a photographic memory, but they respected him no less for going to the bother of addressing each person by name. In a large organisation the boss can hardly be expected to remember everyone anyway.

As long as you remember the names of those you have regular contact with, or clients and colleagues who merit special attention, you will rarely be marked down for the odd memory lapse.

Having said that, it is preferable to master the specific mental skills you have learnt. You never know who you will meet who could turn out to be important to your future. Nor will you ever know what opportunities you may have missed for want of simple memory skills. Sometimes circumstances or shortage of time may preclude a written system. And in any case the methods you are now learning require little effort, and will soon become second nature.

So use both creativity and common sense when you want to remember people. Apply the memory techniques according to the circumstances. Once you have gained confidence in your ability, you can use written or other memory aids to **complement** rather than replace important, innate memory skills.

(4) **USING NAME SOUNDS**

You also need to pay attention to the sound of a name in order to create a dependable memory. The sound of a name will often suggest a meaning that you would not notice from the spelling (English spellings can be very different from the sounds). For instance, Cheney (which you met earlier) sounds like 'chain knee', which you can easily picture. Similarly:

- **Douglas** (dug, glass)

- **Burnett** (burn, net)

- **Tracy** (tray, see or C)

- **Mintz** (mince)

A near match is all you need. So Fleming might suggest 'flaming', Duncan 'drunken', and so on.

In Chapter 3 you met some words without a meaning. Let's see these again:

Crift

Jerv

Sarll

Pebe

Hial

These illustrate just how hard it is to remember names without an obvious or easy meaning. This time (for words in the third main category), you need to **look** for meaning in the name you hear, because a meaning does not come automatically. However, it need neither be literal, sensible, logical or even 'possible' – just **imaginable**.

Let's take the first meaningless word, Crift, and give it a meaning. In this case a similar-sounding word that **does** have meaning will help you to bridge the meaning gap. For example, Crift is close to craft, crypt, croft, Crufts (the dog show), drift, rift (valley), quiffed, thrift.

If any of these similar words has meaning for you, they will remind you of 'Crift'. You can make the association more accurate by adding imagery. For instance, you can add the letter, 'I' to craft (e.g. as the mast of a ship), 'F' to crypt, 'C' to your rift association and so on. In practice you probably won't need the extra memory peg, as you only need a clue, and simply giving attention to the name ensures the link back to it. But the added imagery is no harder on your memory and it might initially give you more confidence in the technique. In any event, by creating a meaning you can associate with an otherwise meaningless name, the name will be far easier to remember.

Look at the other words in the list above and give each a meaning using the same process. The more you think about each name, the more likely you are to think of a meaning. In some cases you will need to stretch your imagination. But you can improve your imagination anyway by **practising** right-brain visualisation of this sort. So it gets easier all the time.

Hopefully you will not meet many names as meaningless as these (although I found a Sarll in the local telephone directory). So if you couldn't come up with any association, don't worry. You will have overcome your memory problem long before you require that level of mental skill.

As you start putting your memory skills into practice, you

will realise how even the most obscure link will give a name meaning. You will also start to trust your memory more, as you realise your natural memory powers, and clock up a few successes. Even more important, you will boost your 'remembering names' self-image – which is often half the problem anyway.

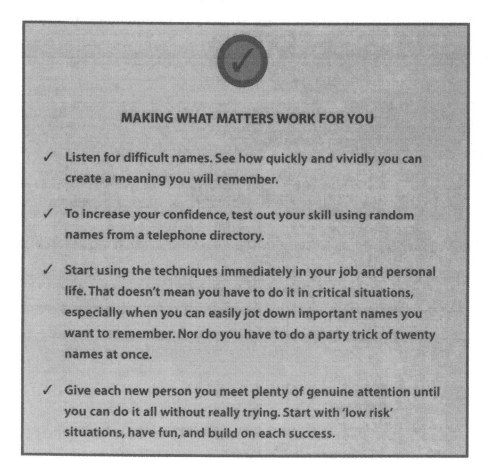

MAKING WHAT MATTERS WORK FOR YOU

✓ Listen for difficult names. See how quickly and vividly you can create a meaning you will remember.

✓ To increase your confidence, test out your skill using random names from a telephone directory.

✓ Start using the techniques immediately in your job and personal life. That doesn't mean you have to do it in critical situations, especially when you can easily jot down important names you want to remember. Nor do you have to do a party trick of twenty names at once.

✓ Give each new person you meet plenty of genuine attention until you can do it all without really trying. Start with 'low risk' situations, have fun, and build on each success.

7 Making Funny Faces

Now you can learn to link the name meaning to a special face feature, and thus recall a name from a face.

Few people have a problem with remembering faces. It's usually putting a name to a face that is difficult. People often say, 'I'm sure we've met somewhere, but I just can't put a name to your face'. Or you meet an old acquaintance and, as you embarrassingly stammer out the smalltalk, you desperately try to remember their name. The harder you try, the worse it gets.

Unlike remembering people's names, we all have a special, in-built ability to recognise faces. Our visual sense is the one we use most in representing the 'real', outside world, and it also dominates our thoughts, imagination and memory. Our awesome sense of vision really comes into its own in the way we recognise fellow human faces.

① USING YOUR FACE-RECOGNISING ABILITY

For present purposes, you don't need to understand these amazing brain processes. You just need to harness the system. You have more than enough brainpower for all the memory accomplishments you are likely to aspire to.

In experiments, people were able to pick out one or two faces that they had never seen before from a hundred or more 'familiar' faces that were often on television and in the media. In many cases they could not quickly put a name to the familiar face, but they knew they had seen it before. And they were just as sure that they had never seen the few strange faces.

Every familiar face is meticulously stored in our brain in such a way that we can identify it immediately, from different angles, when partly obstructed from view, and in a crowd of hundreds. Brain scans show distinctive neural activity when we see faces, as compared with when we hear names. Amazingly, they also reveal a different kind of brain response to unknown and to familiar faces. A wide range of activity, on both sides of the brain, seems to be associated specifically with face recognition.

So far, you have learnt how to remember any name by associating it with a picturable, sensory meaning. The process establishes the vital components of remembering names:

- 'register' a new name

- give the name a strong, 'picturable' association

- follow the basic memory rules whenever you meet a new person whose name you want to remember.

We have seen that most memory work happens unconsciously. For instance, as you look at a person's face and say or think about their name, you will usually make a link, automatically, between the name and the person's face.

You can't help it. The techniques you will learn in this chapter will reinforce that process. But you will also learn to consciously improve your skill at putting names to faces, so that one is always associated with the other. Put another way, you will hang both the name and the face on the same mental peg. By doing this, whenever you think of one, you will think of the other. This requires the sort of imaginative skills you have already met, but used in a special way.

 IDENTIFYING A FACE FEATURE

You need to identify one outstanding feature of a person's face in order to link it with a name meaning.

You will remember, from Chapter 3, that colour names (like Brown or Green) were picturable, but did not always, on their own, provide sufficient meaning. Giving the colour a special, unique meaning (like a white blouse, green carpet, etc) made it more specific, 'sensory', and easier to remember.

In the same way, every face is picturable – in the most sophisticated sense – simply by virtue of our in-built face recognition ability. But you can make it more **specifically, easily** picturable. More than that, a person's face can provide a special meaning that you can then associate with a picturable name meaning. A name will belong to a face, and a face to a name. In an extraordinary way, any face you recognise will **tell you** a name.

Finding a special facial feature doesn't mean looking for abnormalities. Just like fingerprints, every face is different, so there is always some unique feature. The important thing is to choose a feature that stands out **to you**: something – anything – you instinctively notice. You need a 'first impression', not so much of the person, but of the person's face and its features. That distinctive feature will **represent** the person for memory purposes. Just as a slight clue helped you to recall a name meaning, in the same way almost any noticeable face feature will provide the necessary link. Any abnormality will also meet this requirement, provided you keep whatever you imagine firmly in your own mind.

What sort of 'face pictures' provide the link? Each face has a wealth of characteristics when we take the trouble to notice them. And each person has at least one unique characteristic, which is all you need. You have more choice than you might think. There are facial **categories**, like eyes, nose, mouth, ears, chin and jaw (much like the name categories in Chapter 4). And each category has different characteristics – such as the different types of noses, and particular features of those noses.

Here are some examples of what you may notice when you pay attention to a person's face:

- **Eyes**: high or low in relation to the face; large, small, bulbous, sunk, protruding, shifty, close-set or wide apart, goggly, slanting, evil, bloodshot, watery, blinking, staring, squinting, moving, sleepy, quizzical, one higher than the other, dancing, hooded

- **Forehead**: high, wide, narrow, furrowed, shining, regal, lined (one or two lines, or half a dozen)

- **Hair**: colour, length, thick/bushy, thin, high/low hairline, regular/irregular hairline, centre/side parting, covering the ears, backswept, greasy, fuzzy, forward-combed, lacquered

- **Eyebrows**: thin, bushy, dark, light, straight, curved, joined (above nose), shaved, pencilled, arched

- **Nose**: large, wide, flat, aquiline (like an eagle's beak), pug, Roman, bony, fleshy, asymmetrical, broken, red, bent, turned up

- **Nostrils**: visible (from horizontal), flared, narrow, wide, pinched, hairy, moist

- **Cheeks**: high, bony, plump, sagging, full, sunken/hollow, lined/creased, ruddy, pale, classical, rosy, dimpled

- **Mouth**: narrow, wide, full, horizontal, cheesy grin, sloping, curled to the right, curled to the left, toothy, gummy, large, small; notice teeth – irregular, buck, spaces, white, yellow, permanent smile

- **Lips**: straight, short, wide, thin, bulbous, asymmetrical, wet, red, bluish, chapped, pouting

- **Chin**: square, jutting, receding, double, treble, Jimmy Hill (British sports commentator), Michael Schumacher, off centre, pointed, dimpled, cleft, elfish

- **Ears**: large, small, cauliflower, hairy, Spock, full or narrow lobes, close to head, Dumbo

- **Neck**: long, think, skinny, prominent Adam's apple, wrinkled, drawn, dehydrated, mottled, scarred, missing altogether

- **Complexion**: fair, ruddy, bronze, dark, freckled, pale, baby, jaundiced, pallid

And that's not all. You can also check for:

- lines and folds of any kind, from nostrils to mouth, at the side of the eyes, below the eyes, on the cheeks, asymmetrical features

- warts, pimples, dimples, spots, scars, polyps, blackheads, bruises

- surly looks, boyish features, baby features, ugly features, premature ageing, perpetual youthful look, hairs in particular places, sickly pallor.

The above are just suggestions, and are not exhaustive. You can probably add lots more by observing people closely in the street, at work, or when shopping and travelling. Soon you may have more difficulty deciding what to **ignore** in a face than what to notice. As with name meanings, you will be spoiled for choice.

③ **LINKING NAME AND FACE MEANINGS**

Having identified a single outstanding feature, you can create a memorable 'face picture' – a scene, event, image, story – just as you used your imagination to create a 'name picture'. The final part of the technique is to associate the 'face picture' with the 'name picture'.

Once again, you can let your imagination run wild. The association can be as unusual, bizarre, silly, fantastic or humorous as you care to make it. In short, it must be **unforgettable**. Even an innocuous feature can provide a memory peg upon which to hang a fantastic name–face memory.

What sorts of face–name pictures might you be able to create from the many characteristics above? Let's start with easy name associations like the trades and professions we met in Chapter 4 – plumber, tailor, porter, shepherd, etc. In these cases you can think of the person's 'face feature' linked in some way with the name 'role picture'. I have included one or two colour names as well, as these are also an easy type of name to start with.

You might visualise the following name–role images (the name starting with a capital) from the characteristics (shown in bold):

- **a hooked nose** as a Shepherd's crook

- **large ears** as a Porter's hands carrying heavy luggage

- **a thick neck** with a tailor's (Taylor) tape measure round it

- **a high forehead** with a crown on a kingly head (King, Prince, Queen)

- **a 'moist' nose** as a dripping tap awaiting the Plumber

- **a flat nose** with a sawn-off nose (Carpenter, Cutter)

- **a bulbous nose** with a sizzling sausage (Fry, Fryer)

- **an asymmetrical nose** with a Bend(er), Turn(er), or Twist

- **a freckled complexion** with Star(r)s

- **an open mouth** with a hungry Fish, or Swallow(ing) a fishbone

- **greenish eyes** with big Green shades

These are just a few examples. They have now done their job. The skill is in creating your **own**, immediate, outstanding associations.

Use some of the facial features listed earlier to make a vivid, outstanding image. Link the name and face images together as a single picture, scene or story. You can also use some of the names we met in Chapters 4, 5 and 6 with a picturable meaning that you have already created. For instance, how might you associate a flat nose, cauliflower ears, or thick, bushy eyebrows with a 'chain knee' (Cheney) mind picture? Or with 'dug glass' (Douglas)?

You can practise your skills using faces in magazines and newspapers. Start by using a few of your ready-made name meanings. At first, choose easily picturable names, and apply them to faces with an obvious, outstanding feature. Then use actual names from the magazine photograph captions. You can then graduate to 'moving' faces on the television, then to spoken names (or TV captions) and the actual faces they belong to.

The name–face association will strengthen each time you use it. You can use it over and over again, with a standard 'picture' for John, Dickinson, Smith, Gill and so on. However, every face feature you choose will be unique. By finding a unique feature in every face you meet, you ensure that the **connection**, or association, between name and face, will also be unique.

Here are some examples, using a name from each of the three name categories you met earlier, and starting with a couple of 'nose' cases.

A NAME WITH AN IN-BUILT MEANING

Jane Hoover. You immediately notice that Jane has a slightly prominent nose. Make it stretch to the carpet like a (Hoover) vacuum cleaner extension. Hear the loud noise (remember the importance of multi-sensory memories). Imagine holding the elongated nose, like using the rubber vacuum cleaner extension (to add a tactile element). Smell the dust. From now on, that noticeable but otherwise innocent nose will always create the same mind picture, which will instantly remind you of the same bizarre 'hoover' scene and thus the name Hoover.

A FAMILIAR NAME

Viv Palmer. Viv's nose is quite round and pimpled, a bit like a golf ball. See Arnold Palmer (the famous golfer) whacking the nose (it's OK – it's just a golf ball) with a five iron. Or maybe Viv's face is rough and blotchy. Imagine rubbing Palm (or is it Palm Olive?) soap or face cream into his face. Or perhaps his thick hair flops down over his brow. Imagine his hair as palm tree leaves blowing in the wind on his forehead. Maybe Viv is almost bald – his head rather like a coconut. You've got the idea . . . you can start to make your own silly connections.

A NAME WITH NO MEANING

Miss Haswell. So that you can build on what you have already learnt, I'll use the Haswell example we met in Chapter 6. You remember we used the 'well' part of the name to give it a picturable meaning. All that remains is to associate a face feature with the 'well' meaning. For example:

- **sandy-coloured hair** with a well in the desert

- an **oily face** with an oil well

- a **'not well' complexion** with a 'get well' greeting card worn like a party hat, or a 'get well' sticker on the pallid brow of a disinterred body

- **staring eyes** with large eyes staring up from a dark, bottomless well

- **mousy features** with mice scampering headlong into a well

- **spots or freckles** with wells seen from the sky scattered around a desert

- a **tearful look** with tears 'welling up' like a geezer, an overflowing oil well, inkwells in place of eyeballs

and so on. The trick is to make everything vivid, bizarre, over the top, silly, humorous – the sorts of images you can't forget. We don't forget a larger-than-life personality, or a colourful character. Larger-than-life name–face associations are just as powerful.

 MOVING IMAGES

Moving meanings are the most memorable. You can make the association more memorable by adding action, or a little scene or story. For example, from the face features shown in bold:

- a **Tarzan-haired** Mr Bridges swinging from a rope bridge

- a Miss Bridges, hanging from a high bridge by her **well developed teeth**

- Ms Bridges' **staring eyes** with 6-inch optical antennae boasting egg-sized eyeballs joined by a bridge of string

If your intuitive pictured scene changes a bit each time you think of it (perhaps adding an extra, more ludicrous twist), don't worry. That's just your imaginative brain doing its job. The most recent image you have created will be the vital memory peg, just like a last-saved computer file. You can also **consciously** change your face–name mind picture to make it more outstanding, just as you changed a name picture.

Now that you have learnt the special face association techniques, you can adapt or add to the basic rules you learnt in Chapter 1 to incorporate this important stage:

- Look for a prominent face feature even before you hear a person's name, so that you are ready to make a quick association.

- While you are saying or thinking the name (repetition, repetition, repetition) see your memorable name–face mind scene again.

- As you use the name on parting, create a single, final, vivid mental picture that will hang permanently on its own mental peg.

Making really funny faces takes a little effort at first. Most things (like driving a car or knitting) take time to master. But it will soon become second nature, and enjoyable. In most cases you will have several seconds, or a minute or so to make the picture, depending on the circumstances in which you meet the new person. But that's a long time for your intuitive brain to do its job. You may be surprised at how quickly you will be able to do this.

These observation and memory techniques will help you, not just in remembering names and faces, but in many other aspects of your life. You can apply the principles you have learnt in any kind of communication to get your message imprinted in people's memory – in selling, giving presentations or speeches, advertising, writing reports, teaching and training.

As a learner yourself, you can also apply the principles to easily remember what you otherwise may not have retained for five minutes. You will soon start to trust your own brainpower to achieve far bigger goals, whilst enjoying greater self-esteem and confidence. By applying the specific rules and techniques you have learnt, you can improve your people-remembering skills to whatever level you desire.

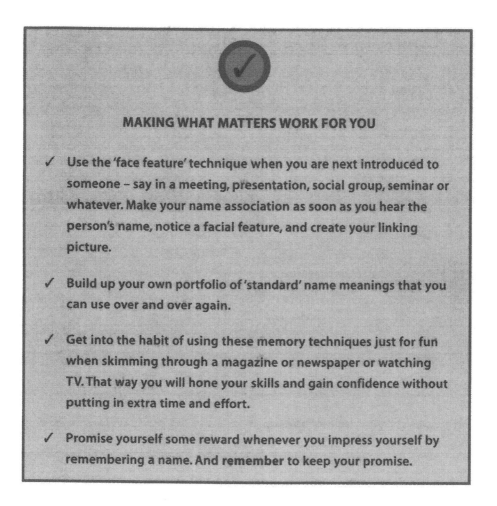

MAKING WHAT MATTERS WORK FOR YOU

✓ Use the 'face feature' technique when you are next introduced to someone – say in a meeting, presentation, social group, seminar or whatever. Make your name association as soon as you hear the person's name, notice a facial feature, and create your linking picture.

✓ Build up your own portfolio of 'standard' name meanings that you can use over and over again.

✓ Get into the habit of using these memory techniques just for fun when skimming through a magazine or newspaper or watching TV. That way you will hone your skills and gain confidence without putting in extra time and effort.

✓ Promise yourself some reward whenever you impress yourself by remembering a name. And remember to keep your promise.